OBSERVATIONS

It's not what ,but how you perceive

VINAV KUMAR SHARMA

Sometimes, carrying on just carrying on, is the superhuman achievement.

Albert camus

DEDICATED TO THE CREATOR, MY PARENTS, FRIENDS, RELATIVES AND EVERYONE WHOM I HAVE LIVED WITH

On Time

- This is kind of subtle thing to think about , if someone dies in an accident or gets injured ,would that person face the same result if he/she had been at some other place at same instant of time.

On Death

- May be we don't realize or we are so entangled by the illusion of life that we forget the fact that each day we are moving closer to the day we will perish.

On Consistency

- Observe deeply the surroundings around you ,each thing you see be it any materialistic thing or the nature , is a result of consistent hard work ,in case of material things ,it is a result of your hard work , in case of surroundings its a result of nature's hard work.

On Importance

- The person who is of true value to you is the one whose deeds , words or actions gave you a deep respite and a purpose to stand during the roughest moments of your life ,it can be your parents ,friends , relatives, a stranger and in a very rare case if you are blessed that person can be the word mentioned at ninth ,nineteenth and fifty first places in this paragraph.

On Conscience

- You can fool your mind but if you are a truly honest human being you can never fool your conscience.

On Love

- Stereotypically the notion of love has been confined to the opposite gender ,where as in reality it can be practised with countless things like our craft ,some habit, some goal, nature it can comprise anything that emanates from your true self

On Corruption

- The most clear definition of corruption is an individual not giving his or her true effort to the work assigned or voluntarily taken by him or her.

On Nature

- One thing which is very profound to think and is of deep relief is that the nature surroundings us, which in turn is encompassed by the universe is not corrupt ,not a single day in my life have i witnessed that something has changed in the patterns of mornings, days, nights ,seasons something which is consistently consistent ,i shudder to think that what would happen if it was nature's nature to be corrupt.

To Know Somebody

- I think it is very difficult to know an individual completely ,his/her surroundings different ,experiences different ,perception different ,beliefs different , in short his /her whole view of reality different ,the only way to know them is crawling inside their body and see the world through their viewpoint and that is not possible so we can say that in general matters we can only practise acceptance to get along ,but yes to get to know about their grip on reality you can ask them just some questions on fundamentals underlying the working of our planet or some basic physics ,you will definitely get to know one thing that is whether they think logically or wishfully.

Nothing Is Permanent

- That saying nothing is permanent is a bit contradictory and the reason is the only way you can feel pain is if you have felt joy at first place that too for a long period of time ,initial years of prosperity when replaced by latter years of pain make sense but i have some doubts about the life where initial years were of pain ,where do those who suffered in those years find a will to carry on because they don't have any joyful experience to wait for and life is a real struggle everyday for such people ,coming back to saying nothing is permanent ,considering the billion years of history of planet earth and to a much lesser extent the advent of civilization ,we humans get to live up to 100 years that too exceptions now here if something lasts for years can be considered permanent whether it is joy or pain and sometimes it becomes real hard to find meaning during times of pain.

On Prosperity

- Too much prosperity deludes our vision of life ,pain is an essential ingredient to keep ourselves grounded.

Altruism

- Excess of money has only two good uses one it grants you life years longer than the limit of human body which is impossible other it is used for the betterment of the one's who had no hand in helping you to earn it.

Something Rare

- If you were given something rare to endure, remember you are fore fitted to be given something rare to enjoy.

Reward Based Theory

- Growing up in a middle class family two things impinged on the conscience, during prosperous times it was the reward that was being given by the family members or society for following certain norms, example score good in school you will get this ,during testing times it was the fear of sustainability of former times as well as inner drive to continue and remembrance of pleasure of former times that gave the fuel to continue living ,the side effect of all this pattern followed for the years was that i had started to see life according to theory which i term up as reward based theory which can be understood in simple terms as doing the work not for the sake of doing or the fulfilment you feel while doing it instead doing it only for the reward you are going to get after you have done it, whether you enjoy it or not, is substituted by the rewards that you get example money that brings you the power of having anything whether you actually want it or not , in all this reward based theory was the crux of the problem which was to be replaced by the pattern that my work is going to be the only reward and the other things are by products in which the only things that matter are my basic needs.

Underlying Dynamics

- The world outside is not as bad as we imagine it to be all it's happenings and workings are only taking place because we are dependent on each other ,and that means we are helping each other that help may have been transformed into a value in terms of money with the changing times but the underlying dynamic remains same ,negative media to some extent robs us of our rational and positive thinking but the truth was and will always remain the same that is world is a beautiful place with us people all roaming around who may not look beautiful but are beautiful from inside.

Being Clever

- Give people what they want to hear not what you wish to tell them.

The Web

- Sometimes visual beauty is a trap.

Virtues and Vices

- The things which have long lasting positive effect in our lives are hard to practise and the one's which require very less effort are just like temptations hard to resist but giving momentary pleasure and regret a long term effect.

On Change

- We humans only change when we are challenged to a limit.

On Transition

- Pain is an essential ingredient for one to turn into a philosopher.

Parents

- Parents can be defined as ,there is a bottle of juice whose lid is too hard for you to open in turn to enjoy the juice parents are the people who put all their energy to open that lid and give you the bottle at the time when it requires minimal effort on your part to open the bottle to make you feel that it was all your labour in some rare cases they even open up the lid for you to see you enjoy the delight.

Love for the Craft

- Anything that we see that feels soothing to our eyes or our conscious being is a result of somebody's consistent hard work labour and love for the work for a longer period of time.

Suffering, Joy, Endurance and Acceptance

- Suffering means suffering it cannot be shortened on our will or by our actions the time that it is going to take is fore fitted , with time we only get to a point where we learn how to negotiate it and negotiating here does not means that we stop feeling the feeling of pain that comes along ,it's just our nervous systems internalize the patterns , pain is always there what you have developed is endurance ,the earlier panic zone of your conscious is now the zone where you have learned how to survive, the world around you impinges you with an utterly false belief of cheering up ,being happy and other things that are said to lighten you up but that's all lies only way to make some peace with testing times or sufferings is to have acceptance which is a hard thing to inculcate, but it will act as an armour to the harmful actions that you will try to take in the defiance of the situation to suppress your ego and that is really dangerous .Sometimes it is better to accept that something's are not in our control and yes the biggest trap is that we feel some kind of materialistic achievement would alleviate the suffering no it would not it may give momentary happiness but the suffering will remain so always remember joy means joy and suffering means suffering irrespective of you like it or not.

On Success

- One of the by products of success is hidden enemies.

The Denial

- Running from suffering is like running from death we know it inside that we have to face it someday but we don't want to admit it to ourselves.

Being Our Trueselves

- We start being who we are when we stop approaching other people with a pre requisite of lasting a good impression on them.

The Cost

- There is a price to be paid for greatness, price which you would not dare to pay even if you get to know in advance that it leads to greatness.

On Journey

- All that you need to figure out while traversing through life is which pleasures you need to avoid.

True Colours

- Everyone behaves as a saint in the crowd to ascertain or fathom some one's true character see what he/she does when they are alone.

Art of Living

- Thinking is the only thing that makes a difference between what's superficial and what is real and often the process to reorient after getting down to truth and practicality of things around you on which you have consciously or unconsciously structured your life is like pulling out a nail out of a wooden board with bare hands which was once hammered with all the effort of your own will and your own hands.

Cost of a Change

- When it is about a change that would not manifest itself into monetary benefits ,only inner growth and refinement, in between the process to inculcate the habits related to change you will have face off with a situation that is you will find that it's not the task that is actually easy or difficult ,it is the practising of that change everyday which offers great resistance to your earlier ways of doing things at that instant of time.

Obstacle

- Adversity struck me in my life as an impediment to the blunder i was structured to commit.

Wisdom

- For a wise man adversity is a brush up with the reality to which he is incapacitated to pay attention during the times of prosperity ,the best use of adversity is made by the one who leverages it to his own advantage by first of all deliberately identifying his flaws and then takes actions judiciously to rectify them and in turn to bring in to result a life of greater fulfilment.

On Growth

- When transition comes things become unstable ,that's why growth is often regarded as a pain full process.

Reason Above All

- Blessed is the man who while facing adversity keeps trudging the way by balancing it with the prosperous times of his life ,since he is a sharp observer of himself and his life he keeps reason and rationality above all the viewpoints of meandering through life circumstances and situations and this thought makes him rejoice even during the times of adversity that nothing happens by chance everything has a reason that unfolds with time and feeling yourself lucky to be stuck with adversity is close to enlightenment of one's existence.

Getting To Know Somebody

- To peel out some one's true nature you have to meet them as a person of absolutely no value at all.

The Mistakes

- We stop appreciating life when we start taking things for granted and that is one bad habit that gets inculcated in us while growing up.

Magic

- When i go for a run every evening my conscious mind is like run do some body warming exercises and then come back ,the day i miss my routine and that too for a thing that did not actually fulfilled my being what i miss is not the running and exercise i do every day ,it's my interaction alone with nature that i miss and it gets stored in my subconscious everyday while i practise my routine, surprisingly it's also the subconscious that tells me what i missed.

Impediments

- We must not pay attention but when we are free of any kind of impediment like physical ,financial ,mental ,social or the one unheard of we are actually enjoying life ,it's the onset of these ailments which acts as an obstacle to the plan which our minds have hatched for our futures.

Counterintuitive

- More the number of things you find counter to your intuition closer you will get to the truth.

On Equality

- We will see and feel equality in the world when the privileged people will sacrifice their wants for the needs of oppressed one's.

Humanity

- World is going to be a beautiful place in terms of living when mankind understands that for equality to boom in our everyday lives we need to confine our desires only to our needs.

Needs and Wants

- At this point of time in world history ,wants would have to be sacrificed so that needs of all are fulfilled.

Thinking minds

- In context to workings of things around us in everyday lives people with no minds believe that what the media ,tradition ,culture ,convention and religion is impinging on our conscious is true ,one with shallow minds believe that whatsoever is happening around them is not to be questioned it has always been like that and they take social proof as a decision maker of right and wrong in their lives, one who are intelligent and wise know that the leaders of the democracies and other regimes are only about symbolism it's the big brother who is pulling the trigger ,at last it's the enlightened one's who know that we are only the instruments or tools all which is controlling things in our lives is the vibes that traverse through this model of space and time and the discretion of giving power to the vibes solely belongs to us irrespective of the final result of the action that the vibe leads to.

Truth

- Truth is important because it gives the clarity, clarity from the confusions , doubts ,discussions of right and wrong . Right and wrong are perceptions but truth is a law , law of nature or the universe and when confronted with it sets you free.

The Difference

- Oblivion ,indifference and ignorance.

The Other Side

- Pain ,suffering and adversity are the things when they strike us our main line of thought that passes our minds is it should get over and we should get back to our former selves but that would not happen ,otherwise what is the meaning of suffering ? Now we all know inherently that the reason we feel suffering is that we know the feeling of joy to the core of our existence and the difference between joy and suffering is that during joys time is like a cool breeze on sea side that refreshes your being every instant of time and suffering is like time has stopped and someone is applying salt to your wounds again and again and it feels like there is no end ,yes it is very difficult to endure such situations ,but yes there is some other side to pain and suffering ,if you have suffered a great deal of time ,then look back at your former self of joyful times ,there may be things like ego , arrogance ,pride , vanity layered into your personality after suffering they are replaced by compassion ,humbleness, humility ,concern, love, care , truthfulness and many more virtues ,so ask yourselves that do you like the former inflated narcissistic sense of self or the one which you have transformed into now ?and you know what bought this beautiful change to your life (suffering),you were busy criticising and complaining it changed you ,second aspect without no doubt suffering impedes the wheel of life we have planned and it's hard for us to swallow ,how did this happen to me ?what wrong have i done ?but think if you are a rational being do you ever questioned the times when everything ,everyday was the way you planned and on your fingertips? I guess no , so what makes you question the times not asked for now ? do you count how many things you have been fortunate with ?or are you this much shallow that one adverse period of time makes you forget all the enjoyment you had till now ?what makes you suffer is it the obstacle in your way or the appearance of success of other's lives ?and what makes you conclude that one who you see happy around you did not suffered or are not going to suffer in future? the things which you aspired for do you truly wanted them or was it just a product of envy towards the society we live in ? were your true emotions and desires were at play or the traps of ego's ?do you know some people suffered more intensely than you ?somebody's loved one's got butchered in front of them ,someone got a terminal disease ,someone lost their children, do you have any idea that how difficult it would be for them to endure life seeing the insane hoopla that society jumps into while celebrating ?and what you posses now has been lost by someone and you are busy in criticism and complaints about shallow things that don't matter .Are not you having everything that is needed to live a good life or is it all about flash fame and superficial things that matters in your lives ?you should ask yourselves and reflect. Suffering is way more than what an ill natured human being can do other it is one's own plan and wish of things getting scattered in front of their eyes and the world being indifferent to all this it also makes you respect each one of us when you start looking at a person with a viewpoint that nobody is free from this trap yes there are some who take out themselves as better person on other side but not all have that divine view of life ,you need support one of the most important things suffering does is altering your view of life bringing you down from the illusion of superficiality to the things that actually matter to which earlier you were oblivious to ,at the end i will quote Dostoevsky ,suffering is inevitable for a deeper heart and larger intelligence ,so is it inevitable for that heart to acknowledge the hidden blessings inside which leads to a life of greater fulfilment and remember pain always serves a purpose that will unfold later ,suffering is inherently not as bad as you think it to be ,it just disperses the illusion you were living in till now.

Actions and Implementation

- To be at peace with yourselves you have to catch the train of your thoughts the actions that are leading you or making those thoughts take seed in your mind and then a decision on your inner self that does this thought which leads to some action actually fulfils me or not ?Am i acting to my own conscience or some other external influence ,these things are to be questioned.

Conceal

- Give others the liberty to think that you are stupid

End Result

- Take adversity as death ,has to be faced by everyone ,just time form and cause will be different ,end result is going to be the same.

Basics

- Beware of visibility and impact.

On Balance

- It's all about balance on this planet ,day and night ,prosperity and adversity if it is not like that the whole life loses it's meaning.

Working Principle

- Nothing around you is happening without reason.

Self Awareness

- The things, situations ,people and circumstances you like and dislike in life tell you more about yourselves then those things ,situations ,people and circumstances.

Creator's Ways

- There were times when my body gave up on me ,my senses gave up on me, in short everything i had ever lived through came down to zero ,even having an intellect that always made me self aware about my own actions was nowhere to be found ,it was very hard for me to apprehend during those times that which part of my existence lived at those times ,to sum it up all there was one belief that god was the saviour and i would try to never forget that.

On Perseverance

- The question is not this that what you do when you get everything you desired expected and aspired for the question is what you did when nothing turned the way you expected ,desired or aspired for , everything zero , what made you going during those times those are the only things that matter rest everything is an illusion or drama.

Meaning In Suffering

- Reason that why one suffers intensely is because one who suffers less intensely should have a well to draw inspiration from to trudge the days ahead or the moments of despair ,disappointment, fear and uncertainty and the reason former makes his way only and only creator is the one to be praised for that.

Pressure and Time

- One thing that will definitely ground you and make you humble is the forging by time and nature.

Us and Surroundings

- We tend to think the things around us are changing but the things have been that way for ages ,a perfect order actually in our clear sense of perception its we who are changing.

Past Present and Future

- Everything was alright back then ,everything is alright right now ,and everything will be alright in future ,it's difficult but you gotta believe.

Perceptions

- Prejudices and biases are mistakes in our perceptions of others one we think that they have lived the life same way as we have second our ego sensitivity of right and wrong.

On Persistence

- No matter how bad it may look or feel ,no matter what you do and do not, during those times ,you have to keep one thought persistent that all this leads to something beautiful and i will be back.

Training of Mind

- If you are ready to feel uneasy ,uncomfortable ,anxious ,frustrated and many more things ,it means you have started the process to control your mind.

Hidden Reserves

- Pain and struggle ignite the volcanoes consisting of enormous reserves of strength which are otherwise lying dormant.

Prayers

- If you pray with all your heart then there is no need to be uncertain or doubtful about the things and events which strike you or the one's which you strike.

The Process

- Remember whenever you feel the feeling of utmost unfamiliarity with your surroundings ,it's because underneath everything is getting restored back to the normal ,the way it actually used to be.

Actions That Matter

- Better to be doer rather than the talker and writer of things.

Meaning of Life

- Nature shapes us.

The Face off

- Einstein's theory of relativity is vividly and deeply experienced during adverse times.

Desire of Beauty

- I don't know why this desire comes ,but i have figured out how and from where this desire comes the desire to have a beautiful person as your life partner ,in my observations of my life i have been an ardent follower of television , many of my morals ,beliefs used to be influenced by the things i exposed to my mind on television ,but let's not divulge from the point and point here we are talking about is to have a beautiful person as your life partner ,where does this vibe comes from ,i tell you where ,you watch television ,thousands of advertisements seldom having the model as an ugly looking person ,you see the movies the lead roles one of the best looking women (yeah sometimes a magic of makeup but it makes them look good) you see tv shows ,again good looking women ,one thing i am confused about is whether they actually look good or start looking good to our eyes when we see them on television ?i need to figure out this ,now comes the application of phenomenon in your real life ,your friends want to have girlfriends who are good looking they marry the girls who are good looking even my father also married a woman who is good looking though it is another thing that my mother's beauty does'nt runs only skin deep ,but what is happening here , this corruption of mind by the television glamour world to have a beautiful person as your partner friend or anything else makes us despise the people who don't look good it makes us indifferent to see the inherent qualities of a person which run far deeper than that facial beauty and what about the other parts of the body ,below face everything remains the same ,still we get ourselves trapped to this phenomenon of visibility and impact ,where skin colour and features are given more preference than character of the person and it is played in our minds by the media, which you try and emulate in your real lives ,what a shame to our thinking minds that can think and act rational but sadly sometimes temptations wins over rationality and we know that intentionally or unintentionally we give preference to good looking whether they are actually good looking people by heart and character or not.

On Character

- It is quite easy to trudge the paths which have been given social approval and validity ,if you want to test your character do something different and do something alone you will get to know what are you made up of.

Comfort Zone

- Resist the temptation to fit in into the receptive mode and this is the mode where you bury your inner inclinations to get fit into what everybody around you is doing (in most cases not aware why they are doing what they are doing) it's just everybody is doing that and they think it's right.

Discipline

- Inculcate the practising of step by step getting familiar to the feeling of unfamiliarity in the pursuit of the change that your soul desires.

Exposing Yourself

- Move towards resistance and pain they are inherently very fruitful and give you fulfilment ,i will repeat again full of boredom ,anxiety ,fear and frustration on the surface but inherently divine.

Looking Inside

- Before criticizing someone take two steps back and look back at your line of action regarding the thing being criticized if you are a truly honest human being then you would think before talking.

On Attachment

- One of the by products of living on the planet is getting naturally exposed to the feelings of attachment and affection and love happens with whole existence of some being it can be anything ,most important thing is the feeling you get with their natural form of behaviour (human beings), if you confuse the feeling of love with the outward appearance then you are mistaken.

On Control

- When you are feeling that your thoughts are making you feel uneasy ,let that moment pass keep your mouth shut mind is not working whatever comes out of your mouth is not in the coherence with what you actually feel keep yourself occupied with anything.

Moment of Change

- Remember whenever extreme numbness or negative thoughts in your mind are attacking you there will be a moment when everything will change you will not get to know when change occurs but everything will be different in microseconds ,so keep trudging pain is just changing you.

On Acceptance

- Acceptance , acceptance and acceptance is all you need avoid preaching if you are self aware then think of yourself at the time when you were living in prosperous times did you listened to anyone around you, no you were busy in your own world of fantasies and illusions when did wisdom came into your life when you were struck with adversity whenever trying to give some wisdom to other being think of this thing and you will restrain yourselves.

Application

- Stop wasting your time making people understand your line of thoughts apply it in your life it is more than enough.

Light at the End

- More you move towards resistance ,pain and darkness there is a different you ,you will discover fulfilment is of higher level and contentment is of higher level.

Question That Arises

- Confusion is that do people indulge in sex due to the genetic inclinations, social and cultural conditioning around them, for procreation or just for the sake of pleasure which it brings?

On Fulfilment

- Earlier the line of action was influenced by the social conditioning that consisted of doing your work , whether you enjoy it inherently or not and compensating it with enjoying the life in free time ,what i want to follow in my life is that i should not see my work as some burden or duty to be carried out yes for satisfying your basic needs any form of work is acceptable ,but i want my stream of work to be the one that i enjoy , i want to make my living from something that i am good at and enjoy while doing it ,this is what i want to happen in my life.

On Compassion

- Try looking at other people as the creation of the same creator that created you ,in spite of the things you don't like about them you will have a feeling of oneness and compassion towards them and it will bring acceptance at a wider scale in your life.

Avoid and Inculcate

- Patterns of behaviour that you don't like in others are the vices that you should avoid and the patterns of behaviours which lead you to feel compassion towards others are the virtues you should inculcate.

Ask Yourself

- It is hard to inculcate but you have to ask yourselves that when you are asked for some action by others are you doing it just out of the obligation or to look good in their eyes ,what that action is going to bring you does it leads to fulfilment at a deeper level or is it just a waste of time which you realize when the time has been lost, saying no to such things is important to see your purpose your routine with clarity is important ,life is not worth it to be wasted on trivial matters which drain your energy and lead you to nowhere ,practising the habit of saying no should be inculcated before it's too late to bring your life back to the way you wanted it to be.

Ups and Downs

- Ups and downs are understood when after period of ups, you encounter downs take a grind polish yourself and again get to see the ups but experiencing a long bout of downs without any ups in the sight or experience is a difficult thing to endure.

Let It Be

- Don't try to add perceptions to any situation or circumstance that you are going through no name no description just let it be what it is.

Obligations

- I do a lot of things out of obligations just to look good in the eyes of other people even if that means making your own personal loss which actually affects me ,i need to avoid such behaviour to please everyone ,the first and foremost important person to get with a feeling of fulfilment is me myself rest everything secondary.

Living In Depth

- To get influenced or carried away is very easy and then taking decisions with that viewpoint of thinking ,but what actually matters is to dig deep and examine your life that how have you lived ,your positives ,negatives ,qualities ,strengths and weaknesses ,after examining your life by such metrics then take a decision towards the goal you want to achieve and also ask yourself that what are the things that you can actually improve in the pursuit of your goal which leads to your contentment and fulfilment.

Objectivity, Subjectivity and Truth

- Our viewpoint of the world is subjective where as world is an objective place it is this difference that needs to be bridged out for the balance of our lives and it is when you get to endure the life's circumstances and situations in order to bridge the gap between your subjective point of view and world's objectivity that is the time that you are tested ,tested for your weakness to make you as much as objective to the events and happenings of the world.

Reorienting

- My subjective point of view automatically makes me form perception about things which is the basic way or circuits of thinking influenced from our way of living and based on our long held morals and beliefs and principles, in regard to living in short the thinking dynamics and there is always a way to look at things which can be called as a scientific approach indirectly we can call it as a truth ,the awareness that creeps in is i have to unlearn attaching my perception to the things in a subjective way and in turn think in an objective way that is not the way you wish it to be but the way it actually is both in context to human relationships ,work life and day to day matters of life inside out.

Emotional Manipulation

- Imagined reality leads you to some objective truth in between the process there are countless manipulations of mind ,it does not matters if one does not follows the process the only thing that matters is your reaching the objective truth.

Comparison and Reality

- Often when we are suffering in one way or another the thing that aggravates it is our comparison to the people around us who look happy irrespective of the thing that whether they are actually happy or not, sometimes we measure ourselves with the events that take place in the majority of people's lives that is society statisequal to get education at certain age to get job at certain age to get settled at certain age and when due to the obstacles and hindrances which life throws in our way we are unable to fulfil those timelines that makes us disappointed but if you believe in balance of cosmos around you then there may be equal number of folks in the life who are actually suffering may be more than you ,the catch is that the world around you magnifies prosperity to such an extent that truth seems like an illusion but if you think and observe deliberately you will find that it's not you alone who is struggling there are countless like you who are in the same race and on a longer run someday you will look back and say that those timelines were also just illusions each one's reality to their own time zones in life according to which they were acting in life moreover why do we indulge in self loathing that if certain things did not happened the way we planned or hoped them to be then it's unfair you have to tell yourselves the realities and living dynamics of everyone's life are different ,the place and time where you suffered someone was enjoying at that time and place and time you enjoy someone somewhere will suffer at that time on a longer run not all the spheres of life are going to be the way you imagined them to be someday the balance of life will hit you whether it hits you harder or normally that depends but someday it's going to get you and your attachment in depth to the times of joy at some point will make it difficult for you to endure those times but yes you will endure and come out as a better person on other side that is for sure.

Viewpoint and Flaw

- My view of world around me is solely based on the environment i am surrounded by ,which shapes my moral beliefs principles values and my feelings for other people in my life are the exact way the things are happening in my own life that is if i am feeling joyous i want others to be joyous as well if, i am feeling sad i want others to be sad as well and this is a flaw ,we should inculcate a practise to think good about others even when we are facing misfortune in our life it is a little bit hard to do but inculcating that positive mindset is possible, all we need to do is practise patience and virtue to think that majority of other people are also the way we are in our lives.

Priming

- Due to the happenings of life developed an awareness of priming done to thinking patterns since childhood from television ,i now get to know that the television throws a lot of cognitive dissonance and it makes sense during prosperity but during adversity it all seems like brainwash , my being is majorly influenced by what i watch so i need to filter what i watch,restricting it to something knowledgeable and having some practical importance in real life.

Seeking Truth

- Are there any forces in this universe that influence human way of living acting and thinking? are there any laws like laws of physics which apply to our conduct throughout our lives? or all the things are merely our perceptions ,is there any thumb rule which applies to all the living beings in nature equally ? if yes then how can we seek and implement them ?

Rationality

- Rationality in its crude form comes down to one thing, just balancing the prosperous times of your life to the testing times no reason ,no justification ,no excuses ,no entitlement, just a plain and simple acceptance of the fact that i did not questioned the prosperous times that should not make me avoid questioning the testing times ,just like the balance of day and night if one diminishes other loses it's meaning.

Realization

- Realization comes either inherently or from some painful experience, nobody changes themselves on someone's recommendation or insistence.

Majority

- In reality people don't have any clear idea about what they want to do in their lives, so they take actions in line with what majority is doing and the sad part is they think and then tend to believe that what majority is doing is right.

Ranking Scale

- When you are talking about people, the sole reasons here are only two, you admire them because they echo what matches with your own ideal thinking of life you can say the right way in your ideology of life ,the other one is you are talking in a way about them that is making you derive sadistic pleasure , may be you are talking behind their backs ,focussing on what in your perception of wrong is done wrong by them ,the interesting part you don't get to know is somewhere you are insecure with their ways of living may be they have fame ,money ,social status or recognition at a much higher degree than you or there can be countless reasons but just ask yourselves .most of the times you are talking about the people who are in the same scale or above your's in the ranking scale of the society ,because you would seldom be talking about a beggar or some person who is insignificant in your perception and the sole reason is that you think that you are somewhere superior to that person.

Zero

- Always think yourselves as zero, even if you achieve everything you wished for or more than that, this will make you grow forever and keep you grounded as well as humble in your life.

Ego

- Definition of ego can be summarized as an old man refusing to accept that a young boy or man is having more depth and wisdom and a clearer understanding of life than him.

Perspective

- At any point of life if you had a serious argument with your friend or a loved one after which you thought about parting ways just think that what if that person dies next day ,or in future ,would you be able to forgive yourselves for your rigidness ? If you really loved that person or gave your time and attention ,in simple shared your life with him/her ,you will never wish to lose him/her on first place.

That One Thing

- Adversity will make one thing really clear to you and that is what actually matters in your life.

EPILOGUE

All the above observations are my personal experiences, things and events that took place in my life and my perceptions of the circumstances and situations which I meandered through . Most of these thoughts occurred to me during my evening run that I have been religiously practising since past three years , I understand that the way these observations have been put forth it would pop many questions in your minds and I would love to answer all your queries on my email address that is vinav.sharma@gmail.com. At any point in the book if you feel connected to any observation which makes you go this way that yeah it happened with me too I would consider that my purpose of writing this book has been fulfilled. Hope you enjoyed reading the book as much as I enjoyed writing and working on it .Much love to all you people now and always.